sportscene

Swimming

sportscene

Swimming

Sean McSweeney
and Rebecca Sampson
(FIST AIST)

B. T. Batsford Ltd · London

First published 1993

© Sean McSweeney and Rebecca Sampson 1993

Typeset by Latimer Trend & Company Ltd, Plymouth
and printed in Hong Kong by Colorcraft Ltd

Published by
B. T. Batsford Ltd
4 Fitzhardinge Street
London W1H 0AH

A CIP catalogue record for this book is available from the British Library

ISBN 0 7134 7128 X

Cover illustration: Monica Paranello of Italy at the French Winter Championships, Dunkirk 1992. Photo Richard Martin © Agence Vandy Stadt/Allsport

Title page illustration: A flying start by Andy Jameson, who won an Olympic bronze for Great Britain in the 200 m butterfly at Los Angeles. Photo © Allsport

Contents

Introduction

A SKILL FOR LIFE

Everybody can swim if they want to, and once you have learned how you will never forget – just like riding a bicycle! People of all ages, from the very young to the very old, can participate, and the disabled can enjoy a mobility that they may not have on land.

Swimming is good all-round exercise and when practised competently it allows you to enjoy many other sports without

worrying about the risk of drowning. In addition, as you will be constantly reminded in these pages, swimming is a competitive sport in its own right.

This book assumes you can already swim – if you cannot, there is no reason why you should not learn. Just remember; the human body floats quite naturally – just waiting for you to move your arms and legs in the correct way!

Whatever your level of ability, this book will help you to swim better. If you are already swimming in competitions the chapters on strokes, starts and turns will help to improve your technique. Maybe you are a beginner and still a little unsure of yourself in water; the early chapters will help you overcome these problems before you go on to learn the strokes.

Even if you are quite a good swimmer it is a good idea to look at the chapter Basic Skills since much of it is relevant to competitive swimming (the section on breathing, for example). Certainly, if you are swimming just for fun this chapter contains much information which will increase the number of things you can do in water and so add to your enjoyment.

There are any number of ways of swimming, of course – you only have to visit your local pool to see that – and a couple of recreational strokes are included in this book; but we are largely concerned with teaching you the four main strokes used in competition. We deal with the front crawl first, mainly because most people's first attempt at swimming involves an alternating stroke in front of the body, and this can provide a basis for the full overarm stroke.

You may want to study another stroke first, but if you do, please read the chapter on crawl beforehand since some general points are included in it. The section on drills is particularly important because some of the techniques and equipment described in it will be referred to when discussing the other strokes.

We have broken down each stroke into its component parts and then looked at it as a whole; common faults are then pointed out and remedies suggested. Finally, we recommend drills to improve parts of the stroke and overall coordination.

We end with an explanation of all the turns and starts used in competitive swimming and give advice on relays, training, fitness and the way to approach and swim a race. However, whether you are a competitor or not, above all else – remember to enjoy your swimming!

Left: not bad for a land animal. A backstroke competitor powers through the water

Getting started

SAFETY

Being able to swim can save your life, but if you are not sensible when in the water you can also put yourself or others in danger. If you follow the guidelines below you should have no problems. It is worth being that extra bit careful so that worry will not spoil your enjoyment.

Generally:

- allow yourself at least an hour after a heavy meal before swimming
- when possible, swim under supervision or at least with a strong swimmer
- always make sure you are properly supervised whenever you are trying a new skill which involves going under water, for example a tumble turn or a duck dive
- do not take in great gulps of air before going under water
- do not hold your breath when under water – breathe out gradually and steadily and make sure you resurface before you feel the need to take another breath
- wear suitable swimwear which allows your limbs full range of movement
- do not swim in very cold water – if you start to feel cold or begin to get very tired, get out immediately
- do not push people in or duck them – not even strong swimmers

In swimming pools:

- obey the lifeguards and follow the rules which are posted at the poolside
- be especially careful when swimming near diving boards
- make sure you know the depth of water that you dive into

In the sea:

- find out about local tides and currents
- obey the lifeguards if there are any and make sure you understand the meaning of signs, flags and buoys
- do not float out to sea on airbeds or other inflatables easily caught by the wind and tides

In other open water, such as lakes:

- swim only in water which you definitely know to be unpolluted
- do not dive or jump into unfamiliar water

One final important point:

- if you have a medical condition such as diabetes, epilepsy or asthma be especially careful and aware of the strain swimming can place on your body. If you have any doubts, check with your doctor; in particular, if you have ear problems you must consult your doctor before taking up swimming – the solution might be a simple one like wearing ear plugs

WHERE TO SWIM

Undoubtedly, the best place for practice and fitness training is a properly supervised swimming pool. An outdoor pool is very pleasant on hot summer days but an indoor one is necessary for year-round practice. Ideally, it should be 25m (27yd) long and deep enough at one end to allow you to dive in. Find out when the pool is not crowded, or if lanes are roped off at special times, so you can swim lengths without worrying about collisions with recreational swimmers.

In the previous section we outlined the hazards which are often present in open water sites such as lakes, rivers and the coast. However, if you are lucky enough to live near a safe and clean stretch of natural water, you will have the opportunity to swim uninterrupted distances in the summer months. This will develop your stamina and the change of venue will stop you from getting bored with your training.

For team training and for learning strokes, turns and starts you will need special pool sessions and perhaps individual tuition. This is where you can best keep records of your times to see how you are improving and where you can go through a serious training programme. We deal with all this in a later chapter (pages 50–3).

WHAT TO WEAR

Swimming costumes

Swimming trunks for boys and one-piece costumes for girls should be in a lightweight, quick-drying fabric (lycra is popular). If you are a girl make sure that the costume allows you to move your shoulders freely. Some swimmers like to wear a heavier costume when training so that they feel lighter and faster when competing. There are also drag suits which trap water and slow you down. When these are worn in training they develop your strength.

Caps and clips

A lightweight waterproof cap is essential if you wear your hair long; even if you have short hair you might find it helps you move more cleanly through the water. If you are troubled by water entering your nose as you turn, then you can wear a nose clip – but if you time your breathing properly this shouldn't really be necessary!

Goggles

Chlorinated water can often irritate the eyes; goggles prevent this happening and allow you to see underwater so you can perform your turns with more confidence. This also means you can avoid collisions with other swimmers in crowded pools.

Never pull the band over your head before settling the goggles on your face – if they slip out of your hand the elastic will pull them back sharply and the impact can damage your eyes. Instead, hold the goggles in position over your eyes with one hand and pull the strap back over your head with the other. Before putting them on, wash out the insides of the goggles with cold tap water to prevent them steaming up. If your eyesight is poor you can have goggles made up with suitable lenses.

You will need a bath towel and, for training and competition days, a bath robe to put on once you come out of the water. It is also a good idea to have a tracksuit to wear over your bathing suit whilst you are waiting to go in, although your bath robe might do just as well. Open-toed waterproof sandals should be worn at the poolside and whilst showering, as these will help to protect you from the annoying foot infections which can often be caught in swimming pools.

Keep your recovery arm straight! Qualified instruction is certainly the best way to learn correct and efficient swimming techniques

In shape for swimming

2

GENERAL HEALTH

Swimming is very good for all-round fitness, but it uses up a lot of energy – you will notice this especially if you decide to take up the sport seriously and get involved in regular training. So a good night's sleep is very important. It is quite easy to overtrain and if you train when tired you will get worse instead of better. Make sure you fit some easy days into your training schedule, and do not swim when ill or when you have a heavy cold.

In addition, remember the following:

- eat sensibly
- do not smoke
- never drink whilst swimming – about half of swimming accidents are due to alcohol
- never be tempted to try drugs

Top French 200m freestyle swimmer Véronique Jardin takes it easy after her event

When stretching, move into the position gently and hold it for about 8 seconds. Ease a little further into the stretch and hold for 5–10 seconds, then come slowly out of the stretch. Never bounce or push to the point of pain. The stretches shown here are good for the tops of your shoulders and upper arm (A), your shoulders and upper back (B), your thighs and shins (C), and the backs of your legs and buttocks (D)

A

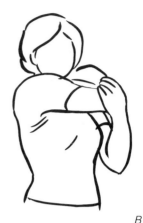

B

C

D

__WARMING UP__

Injuries are not as common in swimming as they are in other sports, and the range of problems is not so wide. This is because there is no physical contact, as there is in, say, soccer; no flying balls or rackets as in squash; and your body is not in contact with a hard surface. In fact, gentle swimming can often help you recover from any soft tissue injuries (e.g. damaged ligaments and tendons) you might suffer when playing more robust games.

Nevertheless, strains are possible – particularly in the muscles – so it is important to make sure your body is warm enough before you set off at full pelt. The best way to warm up for swimming is – to swim! Keep your robe on until it is time to enter the water; once you are in the pool,

swim slow, gentle strokes until your body starts to warm up and gets used to the exercise. Go through all the strokes you are likely to use in the session during the warm-up period.

In competitions you are allowed a warm-up period in the water before you race – this is also so you can get used to the pool, the markings and flags. However, you then have to come out of the water and it might be some time before you race, so dry yourself down with your towel and put your robe on. It is then wise to jog on the spot or do a few simple stretching exercises such as those shown above just before you go back in the water. This is because your muscles will have started to contract and go cold whilst you have been inactive.

FEELING COMFORTABLE IN WATER

We have already said that this book is not intended for the non-swimmer (except that every non-swimmer can learn to swim); so we assume you can swim – however, being able to swim is not always the same thing as feeling relaxed and confident in water. People vary enormously in their feelings about allowing their body to be supported by water.

The right attitude

There are two things to remember if you are uneasy in water:

1 You are not the first person ever to have felt like this – in fact, quite a few of the people you see in your local pool, swimming and diving confidently in deep water, were once as unsure in water as you may now be. If they could change so can you.

2 Confidence and ability feed each other – all you need is the right attitude. Be patient and don't give up just because you get a noseful of water from time to time. And don't let the comments of others put you off – you are doing this for yourself, not for them.

In order to swim at a competitive level you must get used to being *under* water as much as being *in* water. For most people the biggest barrier is the thought of having the whole head under water. Once that is overcome the basic skills dealt with in the next chapter do not seem so frightening.

Ducking your head

To get used to being submerged start by just placing your face in the water so that your nose and mouth are covered (you can practise this at home in the bath or a basin). There is no need to take a deep breath beforehand – in fact this is a dangerous habit to get into. If you can stay under in this way for one second, there is no reason why you can't do it for longer.

As you gain more confidence try ducking your whole head. Hold on to the side rail or the gutter at the shallow end of the pool and bend your knees, bringing your head under, and then straighten up to come out. Do this in a smooth, controlled movement and keep your eyes open.

If need be, wear goggles or a snorkel mask without the breathing tube (check that this may be worn in the pool) to start with. However, you should get used to keeping your eyes open under water without protection – you need to be able to see where you are going. Again, increase the time you spend under the water.

It is safer and more fun to do these simple exercises with a friend – and they can help test how good your vision is underwater. Once you have ducked your head, your partner can hold up some fingers in front of you and you have to say how many when you come up. You can also bend down to retrieve objects such as goggles from the bottom of the pool.

Basic skills

3

*The ability to swim
and glide confidently
underwater is essential
if you want to
represent a team*

BREATHING

When you go underwater the natural tendency is to hold your breath. This is wrong for two main reasons:

1 You will still run out of oxygen but your lungs will not feel it so you will not surface in time. By breathing out you will get the feeling that you need to breathe in again – and this makes you come to the surface.

Even the top swimmers practise their basic skills. This competitor at the 1991 World Championships has a range of buoys and floats to help him hone his technique

2 Competitive swimming is an energetic sport which uses up a lot of oxygen, so it is important from the start to get used to developing breathing patterns. At any one moment in most strokes you will almost certainly be either breathing out or breathing in. If you hold your breath whilst swimming you will soon get very tired.

Breathe out underwater in a steady stream, mainly through the mouth, although you can release a little through your nose as well. Remember to keep your eyes open; being able to see what is around you will increase your confidence and you will be able to stay under for longer than you might expect.

Increasing your confidence

To increase the amount of time you can stay underwater perform the following exercise: wear goggles (or a snorkel mask without the tube) and have a friend at the poolside with a stopwatch (or there may be a clock with a second-hand by the pool). You can take turns in the water but *do not* compete with each other. You are trying to improve your own performance and that is all; there will always be someone who can stay under for longer than you – it is not important.

Stand in chest-deep water at the side of the pool and face *away* from the wall – by being able to watch other swimmers you will worry less about the fact that you are underwater and will not think so much about how much time is passing. Hold the gutter or rail behind you, breathe in – only slightly deeper than you would normally – and bend your knees to bring your head under.

Breathe out in a slow, steady trickle; watch the activity around you. Your friend should tap you on the head every 10 seconds. Do not worry if you have to come up sooner than you would like; it takes time to get used to being submerged. The important thing is not to stay under if you feel you are running out of air.

Next, try sitting on the bottom of the pool at the shallow end. To do this you will need to breathe out quite forcefully because the air in your lungs helps to keep you afloat. Bend your knees to bring your head under then cross your legs in a squat and, as you breathe out, push upwards repeatedly with your arms.

Eventually you will settle on the bottom. Make sure your feet are positioned so you can push off quickly to come back to the surface. You may well be surprised by the amount of air you have to expel.

All of these exercises will increase your confidence in water and make it that much easier when you come to practise your diving and turning.

Breathing one side . . .

The sort of breathing patterns you need to develop when actually swimming are quite different from those above. To get used to this go back to the simple exercise of tilting your head so that your face is in the water. Breathe out steadily through your mouth and then tilt your head to one side so that your mouth and nose are out of the water. Now breathe in sharply through your mouth and bring your face back under as quickly as possible. Breathe out – not too quickly – and repeat the exercise. Practise this until you establish a rhythm.

. . . then the other

You will almost certainly have tilted your head to the same side every time, so the next stage is to practise breathing in on the other side. Once you can do this easily, alternate the sides: breathe out underwater, tilt your head to the right to breathe in sharply through your mouth, place your face in water again to breathe out; then tilt your head to the left and breathe in, breathe out under water, and

so on. Again, this is something you can practise at home in the bath or in a bowl of water, but you will need a swimming pool to go on to the next step.

Stand in water at about chest level, put your hands on your hips and bend your body at the waist so that your face is in the water. Repeat the exercises above (tilting your head one way then the other) whilst walking slowly. Move widthways across the pool so that the water is always at the same level. If you feel unsure about this have a friend to walk with you or take hold of one hand. It is worth practising this until you can do it easily because it forms the basic breathing pattern for front crawl.

To practise the breathing technique for breaststroke go through the same stages as above, but in deeper water so that you start with your head up or only partly angled down, but still under water (keep your eyes above water if you wish). Tilt your head up (not to the side) to breathe in.

For butterfly, start as for crawl practice but push your chin forward and up; catch a quick breath and go face down in the water again. You do not get long to take in air in this stroke!

Remember: breathe out slowly, breathe in quickly – and do both through your mouth rather than your nose.

FLOATING

It is best to float in water which comes up to your neck at least. To begin with, you may want someone to support you at the back of the head when on your back. When on your front you can be supported under your chin or someone can hold your hands.

For most people the natural floating position is not horizontal (flat) but at an angle or even vertical (upright). To find out which is natural for you, start in an upright position with only your head out of water. Spread your arms out sideways and tilt your head back; soon your body will move into a stationary floating position.

Other positions

Once you are confident about floating, switch between the two positions by rolling over. See how many other positions you can float in. Now that you know your body floats in water you will be more relaxed when you practise your swimming strokes.

Left: three typical positions for the human body when floating. Which one is nearest to yours?

GLIDING

When you watch top swimmers going as fast as they can you might think they are driving themselves along non-stop. But, in fact, at a certain point in each stroke most swimmers relax a little and let their bodies glide as the arms move into the next pull. It is also important to glide properly after you dive in or push off to start a race and when you come out of a turn. Basically, you glide when your body is already moving smoothly and quickly through the water and any movement of your arms or legs would only act as a brake and slow you down.

If your natural position is not a horizontal one you can lie flat on your back by stretching your arms behind your head and bending your knees so your heels come up towards your bottom. See how long you can hold this position with as little arm and leg movement as possible.

Front glide

To glide on your front, make your body as long as possible. Stand at the shallow end of the pool with your back to the wall; raise your arms above your head, thumbs touching. Place the sole of one foot against the wall, take a small breath, lower your body into the water and push off. Keep your legs together with toes pointed and hold your arms out in front of you. Your face will be in the water but the back of your head will not.

It is safe to hold your breath whilst gliding, but breathe out if you prefer. As you get used to this exercise you will be able to glide further and further, especially as you begin to time your push-off more neatly. Try it under water as well; as you come near the end of the glide, tilt your head and fingers upwards to bring your body to the surface.

Floating on your front

When floating on your front your arms will be stretched out in front of you and your face will be under water. Holding your breath will make you more buoyant; if you breathe out you will sink a little. Try it in shallow water first: lie flat with your hands on the bottom of the pool, take a breath and lift your hands up and out in front of you. Push your feet off the bottom if necessary. In deeper water you will be able to find your natural floating position.

Back glide

The back glide is performed with your arms by your side. Crouch down in chest-deep water until your shoulders are submerged. Lie back and push off with your feet. You will be looking at the ceiling and your legs will be together at full stretch. To get upright again, bring your knees up to your chest and tilt your head forward. At the same time, stretch your arms out sideways and sweep them forward. As you get vertical drop your feet to the bottom.

Once you can perform the glides easily, try doing them with the various kicks you learn with your strokes.

DIVING

In competition swimming, three of the four styles start with a dive into the water – so if you cannot dive but want to take up swimming seriously you had better do something about it!

First steps

Start by sitting on the edge of the pool with your feet on the rail. The water you are diving into should be at least a foot deeper than your height. Drop your chin on to your chest and bring your arms forward to either side of your head – they should hug your ears. Roll forward and push off with your feet. Straighten your legs and concen-

The sitting dive. Remember to keep your head down – and close your eyes as you break the water! Tilt your head and arms up to resurface

trate on breaking the water with your fingers first.

Do not lift up your head. Most people who are nervous of diving do not like the idea of plunging in without being able to see exactly where they are going – so they look up. This simply means that the face and chest get the full impact of the water, which is not very pleasant and may put them off trying again. By keeping your head down you let your hands and arms break the water for your head and you will enter the water smoothly. You only need to do this properly once to realize how enjoyable and easy diving can be.

Standing dive

From here you can progress to diving from a squat position or from kneeling (one knee on the floor, front foot curled over the edge). Before long you will be able to dive from standing with knees bent. Throw your arms forward (from your ankles or from behind you as you prefer) as you launch yourself and point your head and arms downward to break the water at the right angle.

Concentrate on getting distance through the air and the water – the shallower the dive the better, but do not 'belly flop'! Develop a long glide. To surface again from any dive point your arms and head upwards and kick.

SWIMMING UNDERWATER

The ability to swim underwater will greatly increase your enjoyment of water sports and will develop your confidence. Most people kick legs alternately as for the front crawl (see page 21) and use a variation of the breaststroke (see pages 28–9) in which the hands come all the way back to the thighs. You then keep your arms at your sides for the glide – unless the water is a bit murky, in which case you should hold them out in front of you. If visibility is very poor do not go under at all.

Once your head goes beneath a certain

depth (this varies from person to person) you will feel pressure on your ears. There are various ways to get rid of this: first try swallowing with your mouth closed; if this does not work, pinch your nostrils shut, close your mouth and blow. If you cannot clear your ears come back up to the surface as the pressure can cause damage.

There are several simple games you can play underwater: get a friend to hold out an arm underwater and swim underneath it; swim between a friend's legs; or retrieve objects from the bottom of the pool.

Remember:

- do not swim underwater on your own at first
- do not take a deep breath before going under
- do not hold your breath under water – let the air out slowly
- keep your eyes open – wear goggles if need be
- do not go deeper than 5m (15ft)
- learn how to clear your ears
- come to the surface in good time

TREADING WATER

This is an important survival skill and can be quite essential in a crowded pool when your stroke is interrupted. It is also invalu-able in most water sports. Most people find treading water quite easy to do. The idea is to have the body vertical and move the legs and arms just enough to keep the head out of the water, whilst staying in one place. Practise near the edge of the pool until you become competent. Slowly push your arms outwards (not down-wards) in front of you and back towards your chest.

There are several kicks which can be used: some people use an action like pedalling a cycle, others push down with each foot in turn, like treading grapes, and the breaststroke kick can also be used. The kick is quite fast but the whole skill should appear relaxed and rhythmic; try not to bob up and down.

Practising treading water

To develop your ability in treading water try the following variations:

- both arms still and underwater
- one arm out of the water, the other sculling as normal
- both hands out of the water, elbows in the water
- both arms fully out of the water, hands over your head
- both arms in water but pushing down and using a fast kick to lift as much of the torso out of the water as possible

There are several different leg actions which can be used to tread water so experiment and see which one suits you. This swimmer is using a scissors action

Front crawl

The basic body position for the front crawl

When done properly this is the fastest of all the strokes and is the one used in freestyle races. There is more room for individual variation in crawl than there is in the other strokes, partly because there are not so many competition rules governing technique in freestyle events.

Even so, you must stick to certain basic principles to make it an efficient stroke. Remember: you are aiming to meet with as little resistance as possible as you move through the water; and you want to push as much water behind you as you can. Your body position is vitally important, so we will consider that first.

Body position

Lie flat in the water on your front; your body will form a straight line with your legs and hips just underwater and your shoulders breaking the surface. You will be tilted at a _slight_ angle, head higher than feet, rather than lying absolutely parallel with the water. Your face will be underwater, except when breathing. The standard position for the head is with the water at hairline level and only the crown out of the water, the eyes focused on the bottom of the pool a few yards ahead.

Some swimmers have a higher head position with the eyes looking straight ahead and the forehead out of the water, but this is generally considered to be inefficient because it causes the lower body to drop and therefore creates more resistance. (To understand this, imagine the way a torpedo moves through water or the way an arrow moves through the air; the pointed front clears the way for the rest of the missile – but if the main body hung much below the level of the tip it would slow down the movement. When swimming, your head is like the tip and as much of your body as possible should be behind it.) However, if you cannot get on with the standard head position you must find one that suits you, perhaps with your head tilted only slightly up – but whatever the case, your nose and mouth must be in the water as you exhale.

The front crawl kick or 'flutter kick' does not go down very deep or come above the surface

PARTS OF THE STROKE

Leg action

The kick helps to move you through the water but its main function is to keep your body position balanced and stable.

Move each leg up and down in turn; start the downstroke at the hip and push down with the thigh, letting the lower leg and foot follow more quickly. Two things will happen quite naturally: first, your legs will bend a little at the knee (this happens on the upstroke as well) so don't try to bend them as you may well overdo it; second, at the end of the downstroke your foot will turn inwards. As your foot comes through to its lowest position, start the upstroke (meanwhile your other leg begins its downstroke). Again, your upper leg starts the move. The heel of the foot should come close to the surface or, at most, barely break it.

The two legs should move continuously in a smooth rhythm with the lower legs, especially the ankles, relaxed – but keep the feet fully extended. Your legs will be quite close together.

Arm action

It is the arms which power your stroke and the action is not as easy as the kick so you must pay attention to each phase of the movement.

The first thing to notice is that your hand acts as a paddle, so keep your fingers closed; however, do not squeeze them together. The entry takes place ahead of the shoulder, the first fingertip breaking the water; the hand goes in flat, at an angle, thumbside first. The arm is slightly bent, the elbow just higher than the hand and your upper arm brushes your ear. After entry your arm stretches out fully and moves down; this is the 'catch' position and from here you start to push water behind you.

The forearm and hand now start to pull back towards your body and the elbow bends so that the lower arm is across the bodyline as it comes under the shoulder. At about this point your other arm is out of the water and preparing to enter. Your lower arm pushes back forcefully towards the knee, your hand just brushing your thigh as it does so. Think all the time of your hand pushing water behind you. This final thrust will help carry your arm out of the water.

The stage in which your arm leaves the water is known as 'the recovery'. The action is quite relaxed and loose in contrast to the effort underwater. Your elbow comes out first and lifts well above head level, the lower arm hanging down. Once past your head, the hand comes forward to enter the water. This is the standard recovery and you should make a good effort at this and only consider other variations if really necessary; some swimmers, for example, prefer more of a straight arm action.

Breathing

To inhale, tilt your head sideways with your mouth wide open, teeth behind your lips, on the same side as the arm which is finishing its pull. Return your face to the water as the same arm finishes its recovery. This is a rough guide to the timing – it will vary from swimmer to swimmer. The natural rolling action of the stroke will help you move your head correctly.

Some swimmers look right back towards the ceiling as they breathe in; this is fine, but you should not strain to do it.

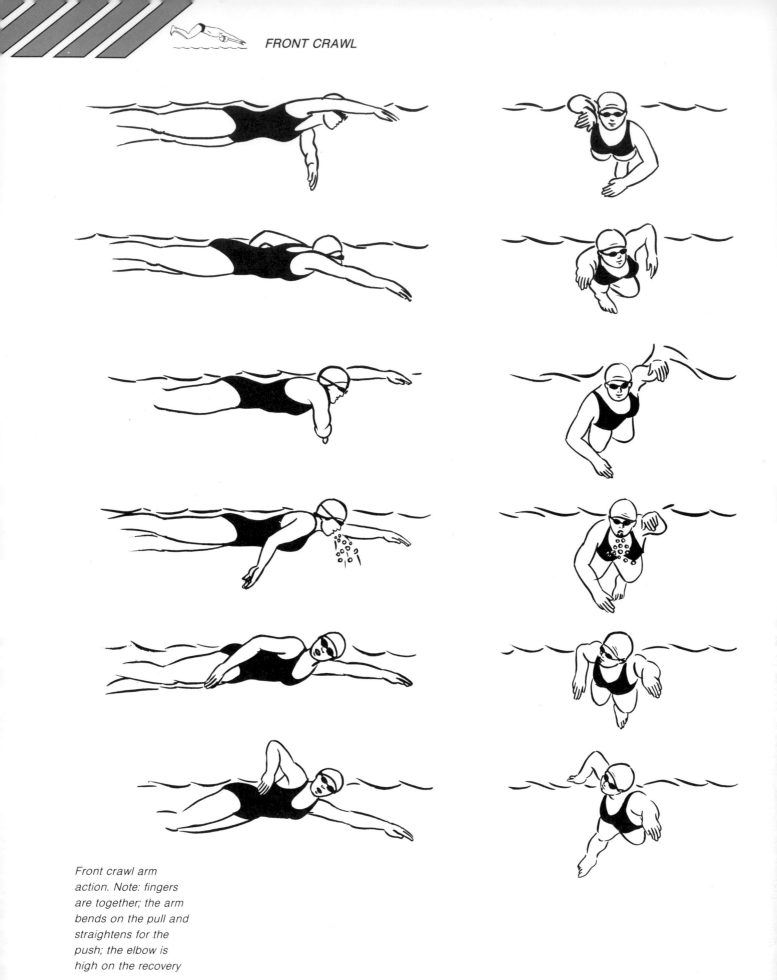

Front crawl arm action. Note: fingers are together; the arm bends on the pull and straightens for the push; the elbow is high on the recovery

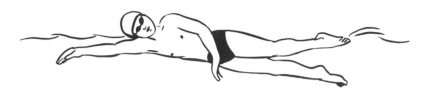

To get a good rhythm the movement should be relaxed, and remember to breathe in through the mouth. Exhalation (breathing out) is also through the mouth, with perhaps a little through the nose. Most swimmers do not exhale immediately the face is under water; but however you time it, all the air should be expelled by the time you are ready to breathe in.

How often you breathe will depend on many things. If you breathe on one side only you will breathe once every cycle (i.e. two strokes, one with each arm) or every two cycles if sprinting. If you can breathe on alternate sides you will breathe after every three strokes; this helps body balance. Being able to breathe on either side has many advantages and gives you more options – for example, it allows you to switch sides and check on the position of all your opponents during a race.

Sprinters tend to hold their breath for a while after diving and gliding, and execute

a few strokes before breathing out and then inhaling. This means that the streamlined shape of the body is not broken for a while. However, this can result in you feeling tired near the end of the race, and you must be aware of the danger involved in holding your breath (see page 14).

Breathing during the crawl: inhaling. Think of your pulling arm as tied to your head by an invisible thread and drawing it sideways as your hand moves back towards your hip. The swimmer below has just inhaled and is turning his face back into the water

THE COMPLETE STROKE

One of the most important questions in coordinating the whole stroke is how often you should kick. The most common (and perhaps the most natural) technique is six kicks per cycle. Distance swimmers often use two kicks per cycle and a four-kick cycle can also be used.

Front crawl has a natural rolling action which makes it easy for you to tilt your head and breathe in; however, this must not become too pronounced or a lot of energy will be wasted.

It is important to develop a good rhythm, which can only come from practising the individual parts of the stroke in drills and spending sessions on the whole stroke. Get this right first before going on to build up speed. Your arms and legs should be moving continuously and smoothly. Finally, remember to keep your eyes open all the time.

COMMON FAULTS

Leg action

Over-kicking: vigorous kicking will not make you move that much faster but it will exhaust you. Similarly, you do not need to kick down very far – generally no deeper than 30cm (1ft).

Foot coming out of the water at the end of the upstroke: this will cause you to move air only, not water; this particular fault generally comes from bending the knee too much, so think of your legs as being straight – without straining to keep them so – and you will get the small, natural knee bend which suits the stroke.

Arm action

Loose wrist under water: at the catch and during the pull do not allow your hand to be bent back or you will not move much water.

Placing the hand across the centre line

of the body on entry: this will cause your body to sway and lose direction and speed. You can easily stop doing this if you watch each hand as it goes in the water.

Hand entering the water too far forward or too near your head: either fault will result in loss of power in the pull. Remember that the arm is outstretched but the elbow slightly bent, and the fingers enter the water first.

Breathing

Lifting head forward to breathe: this breaks the flow of the stroke. Many beginners commit this error because they believe they will swallow water by breathing to the side. In fact, the action of a good crawl style creates a little trough in the water on the breathing side so no water is taken in. Photos and films of top swimmers do not always show this because the trough is hidden by the rest of the water at its normal level.

DRILLS

The important thing when doing drills — and indeed whilst performing any stroke as a learner — is to concentrate on technique and forget about trying to go fast.

Whilst first learning front crawl keep your head up and out of the water so you can watch the entry of the hands; the kick will be quite deep. Then try the stroke with your face in the water, stopping when you need a breath. Switch between the two styles and eventually you will be able to move on to breathing by turning your head.

Practising the kick

The simplest way to practise the kick is to hold onto the gutter or rail at the side of the pool. The float (also known as a kickboard) is also excellent and is used regularly by swimmers at all levels. As well as improving kicking technique, it develops

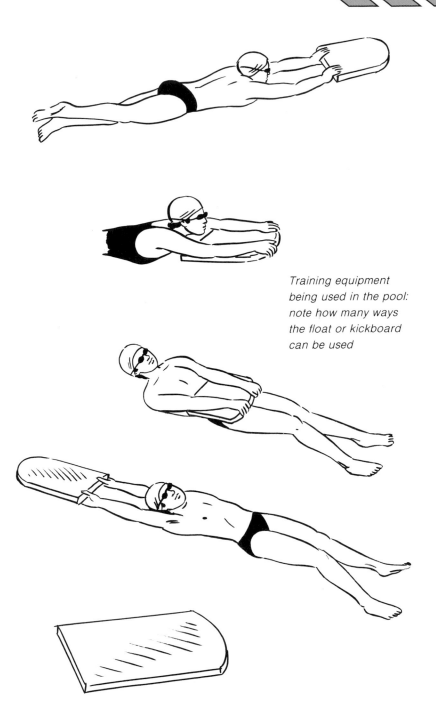

Training equipment being used in the pool: note how many ways the float or kickboard can be used

Far left: the front crawl actions combined in an efficient stroke with a six-beat kick

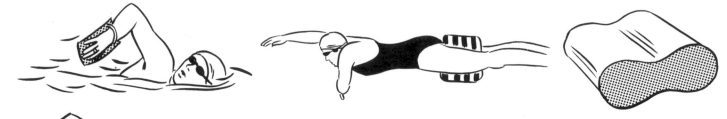

The pull buoy (top right) and the paddle or handboard (above) being used in the pool

stamina and can help with breathing practice. Hold the float high up on either side and rest the forearms on the board. Keep your arms straight and concentrate on good kicking and breathing techniques rather than trying to go fast.

Flippers (if allowed in the pool) will help you develop a nice, flexible action but should not be used very often. Every now and then use the flippers only. Hold your arms out in front of you or by your side and concentrate on your breathing. To make this even more of a challenge take your flippers off and repeat the drill with your arms stretched out in front of you, the thumb of one hand held in the palm of the other. To breathe you will need to lift your head up to the front.

Developing the stroke

You can practise the arm action by holding a special float (called a pull buoy) between your thighs (see illustration above). If you veer off to one side you are probably entering one hand across the centre line of the body.

Paddles (or handboards) are flat sheets of plastic with a large rubber strap at the base for you to slip your wrist through and a smaller rubber strap at the top to take your middle finger (see above). They help you develop a good arm action by naturally emphasizing the most efficient way for your arms to move under water.

Better coordination

To practise the coordination of the stroke without equipment use one arm only and hold the other arm straight out in front of you; breathe on the same side as the moving arm. Do one length breathing

every stroke and then switch arms. Then do each arm in turn breathing every two strokes. Finally, do the same again breathing every three strokes.

In a more difficult variation of the above, hold both arms out in front of you at full stretch. Do a complete stroke with one arm only, taking a breath on that side as you do so. Keep both arms together for a while and use only the legs; then repeat using the other arm.

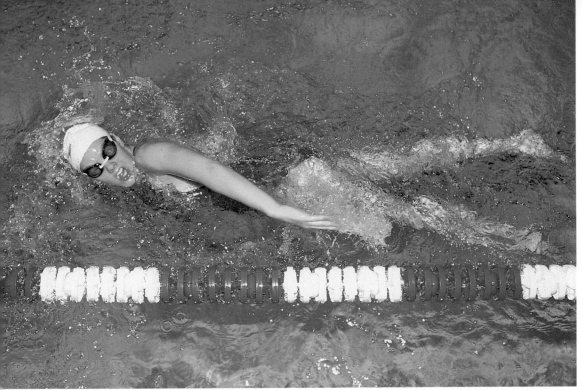

Inhaling during front crawl; even among top swimmers styles vary. This British swimmer in the 1987 National Championships (left) favours a backward tilt of the head, whilst Véronique Jardin (below) breathes in quite late – her arm is about to enter the water

Breaststroke 5

This is a very popular stroke but it is one of the easiest to perform badly. Many swimmers use a wide arm pull and do not get as much forward motion as they could; a sloppy or uneven kick will also mean a lot of energy is wasted.

Body position

In the glide position the body is almost horizontal with only the top of the head out of the water; the legs are straight and together, and the arms are stretched out in front with a slight elbow bend, the thumbs of the hands touching. The position of the trunk should not change much during the stroke but the head, arms and legs will move as described below.

The basic body position for the breaststroke

PARTS OF THE STROKE

Leg action

Both legs move together so that each is a mirror image of the other. The heels separate and come up to the bottom about hip-width apart, with the feet brought up above the knees. The feet turn outwards and push back and outwards in a circular movement which ends up with the feet together and toes pointed away from the body for the glide. A great deal of the power in breaststroke comes from the leg action so be conscientious in practising your drills. Errors in the kick can lead to you being disqualified from a race.

Arm action

The arms make the same movements at the same time. From the glide, your hands turn palm out, angled slightly downwards with the fingers together for the catch. Bend your hands outwards at the wrist to start the pull, which is wide to begin with and back down towards the body. Your elbows start to bend so that by the time the upper arms are nearly vertical your hands are pointing at the bottom of the pool; the angle between the upper and lower arm is less than 90 degrees.

As your forearms come level with your shoulders your hands move towards each other below your chest. Now turn your hands so that the palms face downwards and the fingers point ahead, and stretch your arms ahead of you back into the glide.

Breathing

During the pull your head starts to lift and by the time your shoulders are at their highest point – usually at the end of the pull – jut your chin forward and breath in through the mouth. Lower your face back into the water for the recovery.

Whether you start to breathe out immediately or whether you start to do so during the glide or the pull is a matter of individual choice. However, late exhalation is considered more efficient in competitive swimming. Always breathe in and out once per stroke cycle.

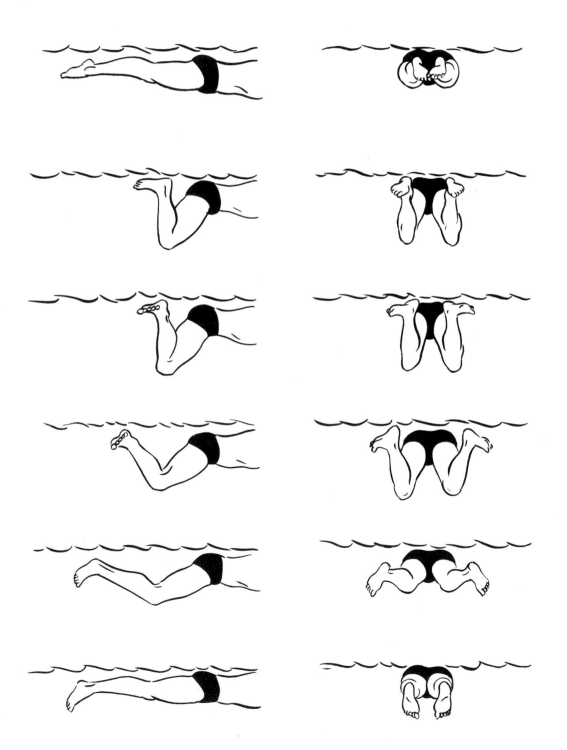

The breaststroke kick can be difficult to coordinate at first so make sure your early efforts are observed by a coach. Both legs must move together in an identical manner. Here we can see both side and back views of each stage

THE COMPLETE STROKE

COMMON FAULTS

We have already commented above on the timing of the breathing pattern. The co-ordination of leg and arm movements is equally important and usually requires a fair bit of practice. The pull starts just before the heels begin to come up slowly towards the buttocks. By the time you begin your arm recovery the heels are in position to start the push. When sprinting, the glide stage can be reduced or done away with altogether. Many competitive swimmers have a high body action with their head and shoulders out of the water for almost the whole stroke – this requires a lot of upper body strength but is not beyond the ability of some boys. The advantage is that you can move quicker through air than through water.

France's Stéphane Vossart, moving into the glide, clearly shows the high body action which many swimmers have now adopted for the breastroke

Leg action

Uneven leg kick: this can only be remedied by devoted practice and use of appropriate drills. You will need a partner or coach to tell you when you have got it right.

Feet not turned out: as above – constant practice and monitoring are necessary. With some people one foot performs correctly and not the other, which may indicate a weak ankle requiring exercises for flexibility and strength. This is important as the more the feet are turned sideways at the beginning of the kick, the more the instep and lower leg can press on the water as the legs are driven backwards.

Arm action

Elbows not bending in the pull: practise the stroke standing up out of water under the supervision of a coach. Then do it bending at the waist in chest deep water with your feet on the bottom.

Elbows dropping towards the ribcage in the pull: use the same correction method suggested for the previous fault.

Breathing

Head lifted up too high when inhaling: this upsets the body position. Try the exercises recommended in the section on breathing (pages 15–16) in Basic Skills.

The streams of bubbles in this underwater shot tell us that Henry Mathers (USA) breathes out as he starts his pull

31

Coordination

Kick and pull happen at the same time: hold the near end of a float in the glide position, then let go to start the pull, keeping the legs straight. Then bring the heels up and perform the full stroke.

DRILLS

At the beginning speed should be your last concern – that will come when you have a good stroke. To begin with you will benefit greatly by having a coach supervise your drills.

Practising the kick

The kick can be practised by holding on to the side rail and also by using a float. If you have particular problems with the action, sit by the side of the pool with your hands on the floor behind you to support your back and perform the movement upside down in the air; concentrate on turning your toes out for the push and getting a symmetrical action, i.e. each leg performs the same action at the same time.

A good drill for the leg action, which also helps your glide and coordination and builds up stamina, involves a normal stroke cycle followed by a second cycle in

The breaststroke arm action seen from the side and the front. Note how the angle of the palms changes in each stage. At no time should your elbows come back behind shoulder level

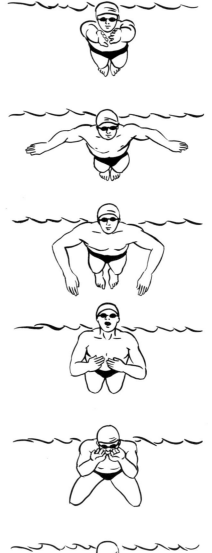

A fully coordinated breaststroke. This swimmer exhales (2nd frame) just before he inhales (3rd frame). The kick occurs as the arms recover

which there is no arm action, just the kick. It is important not to rush the second kick – do it in rhythm. Meanwhile your arms are outstretched in the glide position and your face is in the water. Perform a length like this, one pull every two kicks, and concentrate on your leg action.

Developing the stroke

Paddles can be used for developing the stroke. Using the pull buoy will leave your mind free to concentrate on your arms; it also allows you to practise each arm in turn, with the other arm held out in front of you. Without equipment, you can do the opposite of the two-kick drill suggested above: that is, a pull with no kick (legs extended) followed by a normal cycle.

Once your stroke is well developed and coordinated gradually reduce the glide until you have an almost continuous action.

Backstroke

6

The correct position for your body in the water when swimming backstroke. Your hips and torso will roll as you move, but your head should be kept still

Also known as the back crawl, this can be a very relaxing stroke; and for beginners it has the advantage that the face is out of the water all the time. Swimmers who are nervous about lying on their back should read the advice on floating (pages 16–17).

Body position

You lie on your back, fully extended, with your body very nearly horizontal underwater. Your ears are underwater but your face will be exposed throughout the stroke. The angle of the head varies from swimmer to swimmer, but generally you should have it tilted so that you look somewhere above the level of your feet – not directly up at the ceiling; try to keep your head still throughout the stroke.

PARTS OF THE STROKE

Leg action

The leg action is rather like an upside-down version of the front crawl kick, and, in fact, six beats to a cycle is the normal pattern for this stroke as well. The movement starts from the hips and there is a certain amount of knee-bending at the beginning of the upstroke and at the end of the downstroke. But you should not think about this too much – the kick tends to cause this to happen fairly naturally.

The feet are extended with the toes turned inwards slightly (make sure your legs are a little apart to allow for this). The leg straightens at the end of the upstroke and the toes should finish just below the surface. To get the rhythm of the kick, imagine you are trying to juggle a football using each foot in turn.

A relaxed and elegant backstroke start by Hungary's Kristian Egegszegi, winner of three gold medals in the 1992 Barcelona Olympics (400m medley, 100m and 200m backstroke)

35

The back crawl leg kick not only drives the stroke, it also balances the body – try doing the arm action only with a pull buoy and see how your body sways. A common fault is to perform a cycling action with a high knee; turn this page sideways and note how the sequence should be like walking on tip-toe

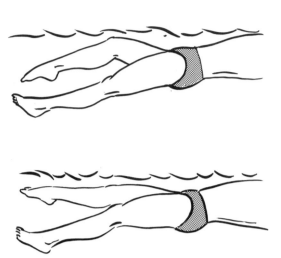

Arm action

Your arms rotate continuously in windmill style, one after the other. The arm is straight as it leaves the water (the recovery); as it reaches its highest point the palm turns out so that the little finger enters the water first in line with the shoulder – your upper arm should just brush your ear.

As the arm comes through the water bend your elbow at a right angle to give maximum pull, while adjusting your hand position to exert maximum pressure on the water. Once your arm is past the shoulder level the arm straightens and moves faster, pushing downwards and then coming up and through with the back of the hand leading the movement.

Breathing

This is the easiest stroke for breathing since your face is out of the water. Even so, it is important to establish a steady rhythm, breathing in and out once per cycle. The simplest and least tiring way is to breathe in as one arm recovers and out as the other recovers. To breathe in use your nose or mouth – or both – whichever suits you. Most swimmers prefer to breathe out through the mouth as this is quicker and clears away any splashing water.

THE COMPLETE STROKE

Of all the strokes this is probably the easiest to coordinate; certainly the more relaxed your limbs are the quicker you will get it right. There is a slight roll towards the side on which the arm is entering; meanwhile the other arm is coming up through the water to start its recovery. It is important that this roll does not become exaggerated – you should hardly be aware of it as you swim. Remember to breathe regularly and steadily.

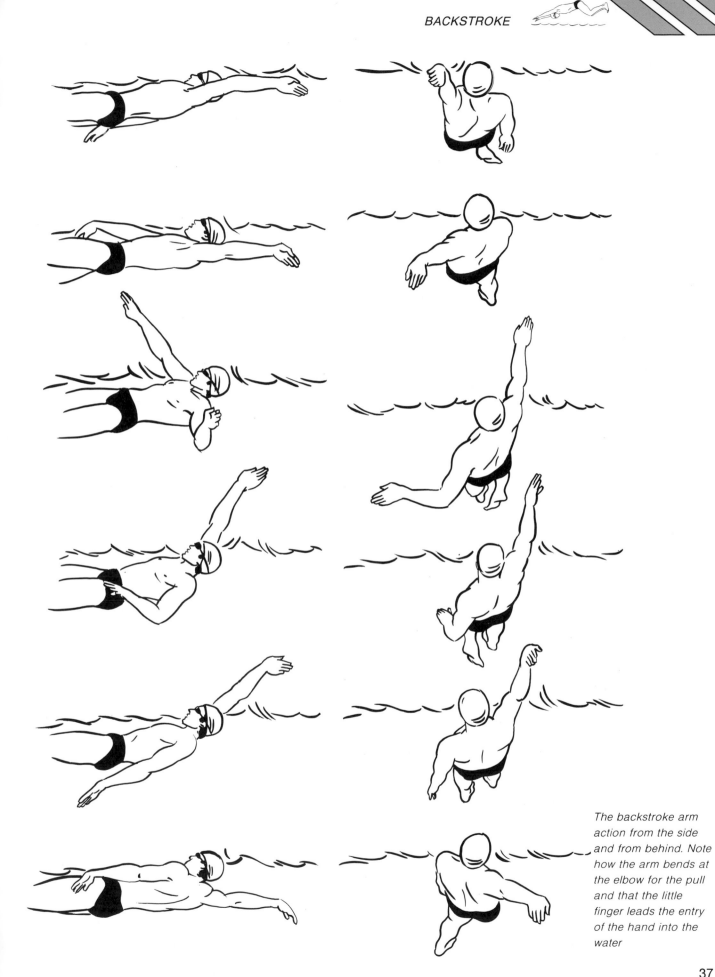

The backstroke arm action from the side and from behind. Note how the arm bends at the elbow for the pull and that the little finger leads the entry of the hand into the water

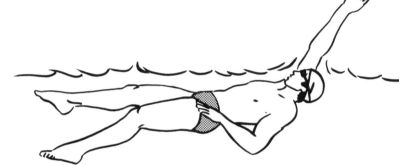

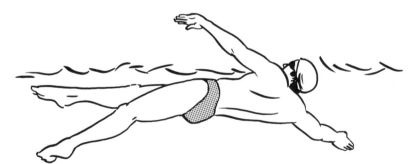

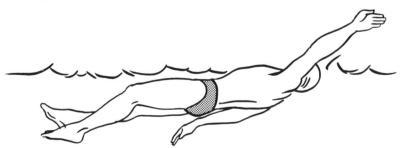

COMMON FAULTS

Leg action

Toes pointed upwards instead of forwards during kick: remember the imaginary football – you are trying to juggle it towards the ceiling, not kick it at your head!

Feet breaking surface of water: hold a float and concentrate on creating a small splash with each kick – but without the foot being visible.

Hips low in the water: your kick may not be strong enough or you may be holding your head too high.

Arm action

Hand enters the water behind the head: if you concentrate on keeping your arm straight and cutting the water with the little finger first this should no longer happen. You can also think of your body as a clock hand with your head pointing to 12. Your right arm should enter at about 11 o'clock, your left at 1 o'clock.

Arm does not bend for the pull: this is largely a matter of practice. Go through the motion standing up out of the water; it is also important to give a downward thrust at the end of the pull to get full propulsion.

DRILLS

Practising the kick

Hold the side rail behind you and perform the leg action. A float, either clasped to the chest or held behind the head, can be used to practise the kick. If you use flippers, abandon the float and fold your arms across your chest. Without equipment, keep your arms by your side and scull with your palms as you kick.

Developing the stroke

To improve your arm stroke, say each phase of the action to yourself as you perform it: 'little finger' (as you enter), 'catch', 'bend elbow', 'push down', 'straighten arm'. Paddles can be used; and if you want to concentrate on the arm action alone, use a pull buoy.

Wearing flippers will also allow you to devote most of your attention to the stroke. Another good drill for the stroke is to perform the action with both arms at once; use a pull buoy if you wish — and make sure there is enough room behind you first!

Better coordination

Performing backstroke with one arm only, the other arm being held by your side or extended behind your head, is good practice for coordinating the stroke, holding a good body position and understanding the rolling action of the stroke. Do not forget to give each arm a turn.

Far left: the complete backstroke cycle with its six-beat kick. Even though your face is always out of the water, it is still important to time your breathing properly to create a powerful stroke

The basic backstroke body position: the right arm about to pull, the left arm starting its recovery, as the left leg completes its upbeat

Butterfly

When executed properly, this is one of the most pleasing styles to watch, with the swimmer appearing to move in leaps. And while it is a tiring and difficult stroke to perform, if you master it you really can feel you have achieved something.

Body position

The upper body is horizontal, and your head is almost completely underwater (except when breathing in), with your face down. Both legs move together continuously, as do both arms.

The basic body position for butterfly. Throughout the stroke the shoulders must be level and square (full on to the end of the pool) and all arm and leg movements must occur in unison

Far right: In butterfly the main kick starts as the arms enter the water ('arms down – kick'), the second starts as they come out ('arms up – kick'). You have only a split second in which to breathe in, at the end of the pull

PARTS OF THE STROKE

Leg action

The power in the dolphin kick comes from the hips and thighs. The downstroke starts with the knees bending and separating slightly, the feet turned in towards each other. Your ankles bend back so that your toes point upwards. Straighten your legs with a quick, snapping action so that the ankles and feet follow through.

The upstroke starts with your legs straight and together; the movement comes from the hips. As your legs come up they begin to bend at the knees to get ready for the next kick. The kick does not break the surface and the downstroke is generally somewhat deeper than in the crawl kick.

Arm action

Your hands enter the water thumbs first ahead of the shoulders, with the arms well extended. From here, you pull outwards and down. The elbows now bend and your hands come down and in towards the middle of your upper chest. The pattern your hands describe is like a keyhole (see illustration on page 44).

Now you push out and back past the

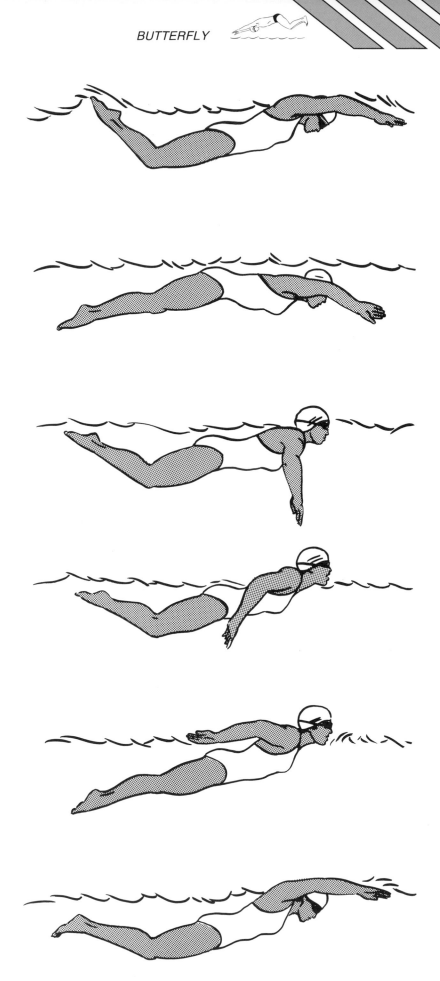

hips and bring your hands up to cut through the water; some swimmers lead the recovery with little fingers, others do so with their thumbs. The whole length of your arms is clear of the water as you sweep them forward and round for the next entry. Throughout the recovery your arms are pretty straight but relaxed.

Breathing

You have to breathe in quickly through your mouth for butterfly, pushing your chin forward as your shoulders rise at the end of the pull. Your face quickly returns to the water and it is usual to start breathing out as your arms come over your head. Since this is such a demanding stroke, it is important to establish an efficient breathing rhythm which suits you.

THE COMPLETE STROKE

There are two kicks in the stroke cycle. You do the first, main kick as the arms start to move down through the water after the recovery. Your hips will be high at the end of the kick and your arms will be moving outwards to start their keyhole shape. By now you will be breathing out steadily. You bring your legs up as the hands prepare to pull backwards.

The second, smaller kick begins as your hands move towards your hips and your chin comes forward. At the moment you breathe in, your trunk and legs are fully extended, your upper body highest in the water and your arms are breaking the surface.

COMMON FAULTS

Leg action

Bending knees too soon on upstroke: do legs-only drills in water and practise the move on land lying on your back or on your side.

41

Pausing before the upstroke: again, land practice can help. It is possible that your downstroke is too forceful. You should aim for a smooth, continuous rhythm.

Mis-timing the kicks: coordination is particularly hard; the tendency is to kick too early. One-arm drills help and you can also hold each of the two positions in the water at which the kicks begin. When doing the full stroke say to yourself 'arms down – kick' and 'arms up – kick'.

Arm action

Arm recovery too high: this wastes energy and reduces forward motion – it is actually easier to perform a low recovery. Lead the exit from the water with your little fingers rather than your thumbs.

Arm entry too wide: your hands should be shoulder width apart as they enter. Practise the move out of water.

Breathing

Rising too high for inhalation: this happens if you lift your whole head rather than just jut your chin forward, and it can result in a poor bodyline with the hips too low in the water. Make sure you are timing your breathing properly – you may have to take in air a little earlier. Do arms-only drills.

DRILLS

It is helpful to have a strong front crawl before trying the butterfly. Do not expect too much progress too soon or you will lose interest – a few drills every session in the early stages will keep it fun.

Breathing

Start by floating face down in the water, feet together and arms out in front of you shoulder width apart. Bend backwards from the waist (the 'start position') and then forwards; repeat as often as you can before standing up to take a breath. Now get in the same start position and bend your knees, pointing your toes up and back; do not let your feet break the surface.

Practising kick and stroke

Next kick downwards from the knee, raise your hips and press your head down; hold that position then repeat until you have to stand up in order to breathe. The next stage is to practise the arm action. From the start position perform the full arm

The power, effort and grace of the butterfly stroke. These three swimmers are caught at the beginning of the recovery. Top left is J. Yves Huguenin of France. Sharon Davis (above), probably Britain's best known female swimmer, prefers to lead the recovery with her little finger. Sharon won a silver medal in the 400m medley at the Moscow Olympics. Another British swimmer, Andrew Jameson (left), surges forward in the 1986 USA Championships. Andrew competes at both 100m and 200m stroke but with a slow underwater recovery. Do not kick or surface to breathe during the stroke. Repeat the drill until you need to breathe.

After you have practised the dolphin kick whilst holding on to the side of the pool, do it on your side in open water with your lower arm extended forwards. Practise the kick underwater and also on your back with your hands sculling. Do all of these wearing flippers and also do it on your front, breathing to the side. Use a float without flippers; breathe to the front if possible or to the side if not.

Paddles are extremely useful for developing the arm action. When using the pull buoy, keep your hips flexible and relaxed but do not kick; breathe in every two strokes.

If your arms are not clearing the water in recovery, switch to a breaststroke leg action until your arms come out of the water high enough. Then revert to the dolphin kick.

Better coordination

When performing the whole stroke, think of the action as kicking the hands into the water and kicking them out again. One-arm drills are useful for tightening up coordination: float face down with both arms stretched out in front of the body. Keep one arm in front and perform the stroke with the other breathing to the same side as the active arm during the pull. After a few strokes switch arms. Now do the same but with the unused arm by your side.

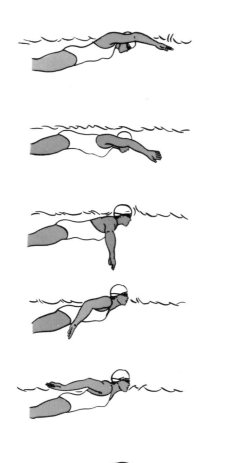

Throw your arms forward so that your hands enter the water in line with your shoulders. Note the characteristic keyhole shape (frame 3) which precedes the butterfly pull

Getting better

STAMINA AND SPEED

As you learn the principal strokes you will notice that, to begin with, you are only able to use them in short bursts. This may come as something of a surprise if you have been used to swimming reasonable distances using your own variety of the strokes.

The fact is that the very process of learning can be quite tiring in itself as you are putting a lot of effort into concentrating on several things at once. Eventually, you will be able to swim further, faster, better and more efficiently by using the correct techniques. Meanwhile though, you must build up your stamina.

Going further

Start by swimming just one width or length of a particular stroke and then take a small rest. Repeat this until you find it easy. Then, perhaps, do the same with another stroke or two – to make it more interesting and to increase the distance you can swim them as well.

The next step is to increase the distance you swim without a break – two widths or lengths. Carry on in the same way, varying the strokes you use. You will not be able to double the distance at each stage but you will get stronger. It is also a good idea to count how many strokes it takes you to cover a certain distance; you will be able to reduce the number as your stamina grows and your technique improves. Be patient though; the whole process takes time.

Going faster

As you get stronger and as your technique improves so you will get faster almost without realizing it. Do not try to go fast before you have really mastered the stroke – apart from anything else, you may make technical errors which would disqualify you from a race should you get involved in galas.

If you have a coach, he or she will be able to pay special attention to your breathing patterns and coordination with a view to increasing your speed. Naturally, the easiest way to monitor your improvement is to record your times for each stroke over set distances.

LEARNING THROUGH FUN

So far we have taken a serious look at the skills and techniques which will make you a good all-round swimmer; if you practise these regularly you cannot help but improve – especially if you get coaching from a qualified instructor. No doubt you will enjoy your sessions, but they will be hard work as well, so it is also important to have fun. Otherwise, one day you could lose interest, and you might not even know why.

Playing games in water and experimenting with different strokes and skills not only keeps you fresh, it also makes you aware of your capabilities and limits in water. There is no need to buy equipment or join special clubs to have fun in water. There are many things you can do with a friend or two – or even on your own. Here are just a few suggestions:

Duck diving: lie flat on the surface with your arms in front of you; put your hands together and bend at the waist so your head and arms go under, then kick your legs up. Pull your arms back and kick to go down. Some pools have objects such as quoits which you can pick up from the bottom.

Depth charge: tread water and push your upper body out of the water as high as you can; stop kicking, bring your feet together and at the same time throw your arms above your hand and join hands. As you sink, breathe out and see how far down you can go.

Crocodile fight: you are Tarzan killing an imaginary crocodile – a good excuse for lots of splashing and wild somersaults.

Handstand: in waist-deep water, place your hands on the bottom and kick up – just as you would on land. In deep water, lie on your back and bring your knees to your chest; fall backwards from the waist, breathing out through your nose as you go under. Then straighten your legs.

Hobble swim: grab hold of your ankle with one hand and try swimming; then switch legs.

Once you become proficient at swimming, the number of sports in which you can participate will increase greatly. Here we see the competitiveness and drama of a water polo match

Porpoise: with your arms by your side or in front of you, kick to move forward through the water and spin as you go so that you move like a drill. Try this wearing flippers.

Water snake: hold a friend's ankles while he or she does the arm stroke and you kick; then swap.

If balls are allowed in your local pool then there are even more possibilities for games. And many teaching aids such as floats can be used imaginatively to create new activities.

OTHER STROKES

The strokes used in competition did not suddenly appear newly-formed. They are the result of numerous changes and ex-periments over many years. Some of the strokes which were popular in earlier times still exist and are preferred by some recreational swimmers; it might be worth trying some of them out just for fun.

We include a couple of them here; they are quite different from the competition styles and so will add variety to your programme. What is more, they do have particular merits of their own: both of them are pleasant, leisurely strokes which are relaxing to do in between the more demanding parts of a training programme.

Sidestroke is useful for survival swim-ming (to conserve energy) and life-saving, and can also be used underwater. There is quite a knack to getting the coordination right, so it will contribute to that area of your swimming skills. The inverted breaststroke is a good drill for the breast-stroke kick.

Another possibility is high-diving. This spectacular shot shows a reverse dive by Tracey Miles, competing in the 1991 British National Diving Championships at Crystal Palace

Sidestroke

Study the diagrams to see how the stroke is performed. As the lower arm completes its bent-arm pull below the shoulder, the knees bend and the scissor kick begins. The top arm bends to bring the hand towards the lower shoulder, while the lower leg bends back and the front leg forward.

The legs continue to separate, the top one almost straightening, as the top arm begins its pull from the elbow with the palm and forearm pushing back; meanwhile the top arm is recovering and the legs are coming together again. The top arm straightens alongside the body and the glide begins with the toes pointed; the next cycle begins whilst the body is still in motion. Note how the head is tilted at the same angle throughout, allowing you to breathe easily.

Try this first on one side of the body, then the other – do not practise it only on your better side! You may find the co-ordination difficult at first, even on your good side, but it will suddenly come together and you will find this a most enjoyable stroke.

Inverted breaststroke

Again the diagrams will help you understand the stroke. Do not practise this in a crowded pool – or you will stand a good chance of hitting someone by mistake! The stroke has a very wide action and you will be going backwards so make sure you have lots of room.

In the glide position your arms are ahead of you, thumbs together and palms up. The head and body position are as for the backstroke. The arms scull together, the palms turning outwards for the catch; the pull is usually with straight arms, but you can bend them slightly if you want.

Breathe out as they come to the sides of the body, and bring the hands up towards the chest. So far the legs have not moved but now they start to bend at the knee, the feet turning outwards, as the hands go behind the head and you take in a breath. The feet drive backwards in an upside-down version of the breaststroke kick. The arms extend fully and then the legs finish the kick as you move into a brief glide.

WHAT NEXT?

By now you probably have an idea of how seriously you intend to take your swimming. If you enjoy the sport but are not particularly fast or do not fancy the idea of racing, perhaps you might be interested in other water activities. These can roughly be divided into two groups: safety skills and water sports.

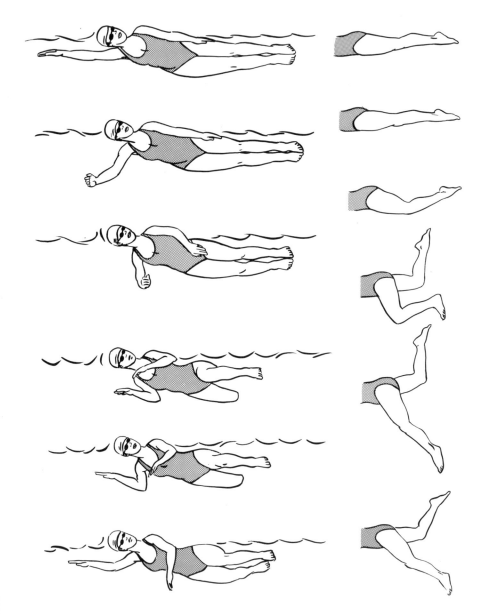

Sidestroke. One arm pulls as the other recovers. The sequence on the right shows the sidestroke scissors action seen from above. This sequence corresponds exactly with that opposite, so you can see how the arms and legs work together

Inverted breaststroke is a relaxing style. You might want to use it to cool down after a hard training session

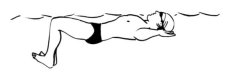

Safety skills

Safety skills can be used to guarantee your own safety in water or to help others in trouble. To begin with you will need to prove you can swim competently; the easiest way to do this is to get the distance certificates which the ASA awards in special pool sessions. From there you progress to the personal survival medals (bronze, silver and gold). To gain these you are tested on your ability to do such things as dive, tread water and swim with clothes on.

Once you are qualified in personal survival you will be ready to take a life-saving course. Amongst other things, you will learn:

- how to tow someone who is having problems in the water
- how to get them ashore
- how to give them artificial respiration

These skills are immensely valuable and will make you a welcome member of any group involved in water activities. The qualification could be a great asset to you later if you ever want to work as a lifeguard or swimming instructor.

Water sports

Sports involving swimming include:

- team games such as water polo, underwater hockey (nicknamed 'Octopush' and played in snorkeling gear) and synchronized swimming
- individual activities such as high diving, surfing and windsurfing
- activities which require small watercraft – sailing, canoeing, rowing, water-skiing
- sports which explore the beauty of the underwater world but which are dangerous if not learned properly: snorkeling and scuba-diving

No doubt you can think of many more; what they all have in common is that, in order for you to participate safely, you must be able to swim well and be confident enough not to panic if you suddenly find yourself with a few feet of water above your head.

Perhaps the activities above only interest you a little and you would rather concentrate on competing in galas with the eventual hope of representing your school, club, county or – who knows? – even your country. If this is the case, the two chapters which follow this one are definitely for you; and even if you intend to swim only for fun you will find plenty in them to give you new ideas.

IN GENERAL

It is not possible to give one training programme which would suit everyone; how much you do and what you do depends on many factors, among them, your age and size, your ability, the strokes you swim and the distances you want to compete at. But we can make some general points about the subject.

To begin with, you should always be prepared to change a programme or routine if you think it is necessary. You must also make sure that all aspects of the sport that you need to know about are included – for example, turns and starts, and the rules for competitions.

It is also wise to do both distance and sprint work, regardless of your event. The sprinter needs to do distance swimming to develop stamina and fitness. The distance swimmer must do sprints to avoid the danger of becoming 'one-paced', that is, unable to put in a burst of speed when needed – at the finish of a race for example. Your sessions should not all be as difficult or as easy as each other – ring the changes. One other thing: make sure you are warmed up before going flat out (see page 12).

A medley training session at the magnificent Mission Bay centre in the USA. Note the marker flags at the bottom of the picture which are positioned 2m from the end wall

PLANNING A PROGRAMME

In addition to the general points made above there are three essential things to bear in mind about training:

- there must be a lot of variety to keep you interested
- you must have suitable challenges: if the targets set are too difficult you will want to give up; if they are too easy you will get bored
- your programme must be planned so that you peak at the right time

Variety is fun

You can bring variety to your training by practising all the strokes – even if you swim only one in competitions. In fact, swimming in different styles can help your rhythm. There should also be some fun in your sessions; if it is all slog you will soon feel like giving up. If you train in a group under a coach put forward the idea of occasional casual games of water polo or water volley ball before you go off to shower. You can also have medley relays with every team doing the strokes in a different order, or all the swimmers being allowed to use arms only or legs only.

The drills you practise whilst learning a stroke are still useful in advanced training sessions. This is especially true of the work done with floats, paddles and pull buoys; they help you to build stamina, to maintain good technique and to improve your general coordination.

As you get fitter and stronger you might include some work out of water. Simple exercises like press-ups and pull-ups (also called chin-ups) can develop your strength. There are also several exercises you can do with a stretch cord (a rubber rope which you pull against) which have the same effect.

The right programme for you

Set yourself targets, but make sure they are realistic ones. Keep records of your personal best times, both in training and in competition. If improvement tails off or if your gala times are worse than your practice times then you can be sure something is wrong, and you will need to rethink your training programme or your attitude. Sometimes you might just need a break but are not aware of it.

Planning your programme so that you reach peak form at the right time is quite a skill in itself. The basic idea is to do your heaviest training some weeks before an event and to gradually reduce your workload as the day draws nearer. You should certainly have a few days' break before a competition. It is possible to overtrain and if you do the result will be worse, not better performances.

If you have joined a swimming club or are a member of a team, a lot of your training will be organized for you; but if it does not feel right – say so. If you are bored or too tired or find the routine too difficult you must let your coach know; then you can discuss it and work out a better programme for you. At the end of a training session you should feel good – relaxed and confident and looking forward to the next time you go in the water.

A specimen training programme

We said at the beginning of this chapter that it would not be possible to devise a training programme which would suit everyone, so the specimen below is to give you an idea of how a programme might be constructed. It should build up your stamina, increase your speed and improve your technique. First, a few points need to be made so that you can understand the programme.

'Stroke' refers to the stroke you use in competition. If your particular stroke is mentioned by name, then substitute another for it. On day 2, for example, a freestyle swimmer would not use front crawl in the repetitions planned in the sub set. The main set is for building up endurance and the sub set concentrates on speed, recovery and techniques. For a distance swimmer the main set would be bulkier, whereas a middle distance swimmer would not do as many 25m or 50m bursts as a sprinter in the sub set.

Some of the training methods will need to be explained:

- intervals are a series of swims over the same distance using the same stroke at a little less than top speed, with a short recovery time (10–45 seconds) between each burst
- repetitions are a smaller series of swims over a set distance at maximum speed with a full recovery period (2–5 minutes) between each burst
- a staircase (or pyramid) is a series of swims in which the distance decreases as the number of repetitions increases

Repetitions are very demanding and not used as often as intervals. The lengths in a staircase may be swum at a steady speed or with a fast 25m alternating with a slow 25m. Take at least thirty seconds rest between each step. You can go up the staircase (1 × 100m, 2 × 50m etc), start at the top and come down (4 × 25m, 2 × 50m etc), or go up and come down.

	DAY 1	DAY 2	DAY 3	DAY 4	DAY 5	DAY 6	DAY 7
WARM UP	• 400 m front crawl, increase speed last 50m	• 200 m stroke very slow • 100 m medley	• 800 m medley	• 400 m stroke, gradually increasing speed	• 600 m front crawl/ backstroke change every 100 m	• 200 m stroke	• 200 m medley
MAIN SET	• 500 m stroke • 200 m medley (race speed) • 500 m front crawl	• 1,000 m stroke	• 400 m pullbuoy medley • 1,000 m front crawl • 500 m stroke	• 1,000 m medley alternate easy and hard 100 m • intervals 10 × 100 m front crawl	• 1,000 m stroke • 400 m kickboard medley • 500 m butterfly or breaststroke	• 500 m front crawl • 200 m medley • intervals 10 × 100 m stroke	
SUB SET	• 200 m pullbuoy stroke • practise turns • intervals 10 × 50 m front crawl • staircase stroke 1 × 400 m 2 × 200 m 4 × 100 m	• repetitions 4 × 100 m front crawl • 500 m stroke • 400 m kickboard stroke • technique drills for non-competition strokes	• practise starts • intervals 10 × 100 m stroke • 400 m kickboard front crawl • staircase backstroke 1 × 100 m 2 × 50 m 4 × 25 m • 500 m stroke (race speed)	• 100 m pullbuoy front crawl • intervals 10 × 50m stroke • 200 m kickboard stroke • team relay any stroke 50 m each leg	• practise turns • repetitions 4 × 200 m stroke • 100 m kickboard stroke • intervals 20 × 25 m front crawl 10 × 25 m stroke	• staircase butterfly or breaststroke 1 × 400 m 2 × 200 m 4 × 100 m • technique drills for stroke	• practise all starts and turns • sprints 1 × 25 m each stroke • 400 m any stroke
COOL DOWN	• slow 500 m front crawl/ backstroke alternate lengths	• 200 m front crawl	• slow 500 m front crawl	• 400 m front crawl/ backstroke alternate lengths	• 200 m backstroke	• slow 200 m stroke	• slow 200 m backstroke

It is a good idea to follow a hard session with an easier one and to have one very easy day per week (day 7 in this case). At a certain stage your coach might decide that you should do two sessions (one in the morning, one in the evening) on some days.

Tapering

Your programme will change as you near competition dates; generally, you will do less distance work and more sprints and middle distance swims. This change, known as 'tapering' should be gradual. You should have at least one full day's complete rest before an event.

In Britain you will do the bulk of your endurance work between July and November. County championships are held about January and the regional championships generally take place in March, so if you are swimming at that level you will start tapering to suit those galas. In addition, you might have club and school galas. A top swimmer might need to build up a little in April and taper again for the national championships in May.

And remember . . .

- go for variety – especially in the sub set
- keep a record of your best times
- keep a record of the programme you have been following
- check and revise your programme when necessary
- do not neglect technique
- consider the possibility of strength training outside the pool
- tell your coach if you get tired or bored

Competition swimming

If you have got as far as competing in galas than you have certainly shown a lot of dedication and you can allow yourself some congratulations – whether or not you win your event. If you intend to continue with the sport at a serious level you will have to show even more determination in the future. As you get older you will do more training sessions per week than at present; sometimes this will involve getting out of bed on cold winter mornings – but if you love the sport you will surely not mind.

It is worth briefly mentioning the variety of events that you might get involved in. They range from 25-metre sprints to 1500-metre distance races in the various strokes. It is also possible to swim medleys, in which you perform all four strokes, and relays, in which you will be a team member.

STARTS

For all starts the official will call 'Take your marks!' and then, when all the swimmers are in position, will fire the starting gun.

Racing dive

You start all styles other than backstroke with a dive from the starting block, with your knees bent and toes curled over the edge. You aim for a shallow dive and enter the water at a flattish angle, your hands entering the water in front of your head which is tilted down. In breaststroke you are allowed your first stroke underwater; for the other styles you must surface first.

There are three different ways you can dive in. For the grab start you hold the edge of the block outside or inside your feet and lean forward on the words 'on your marks'. At the pistol bend your elbows and tilt forward. As you come off the block throw your arms forward and push from the legs to extend your body.

For the wind-up start your arms are held out in front of you, more or less horizontally. When the gun sounds you lean forward and throw your arms back, bringing them vigorously forward as you push off with your legs.

The arm-swing start is similar but you begin with your arms held lower and, as you fall, you throw them behind you and over your head so they describe a circle. As the arms come through you push off the block. Both of these styles are slightly slower than the grab start but produce a longer dive, so they are suitable for relay races, in which it is wise to make sure your teammate has touched the wall before diving.

The tensest moment of any race – the second before the gun. Both swimmers are using a grab start, with Jenna Johnson of the USA (foreground) taking up a staggered foot position

Captured in one shot, all the excitement of the gala. There's not much in it as these three freestyle swimmers race for the finish

Backstroke start

For the backstroke you start in the water. Hold on to the side rail or gutter – in galas you will probably be able to use grips at the base of the starting block – place your feet on the wall underwater at midriff level, bend your elbows and pull yourself forward with your chin tucked in. Your body will be bunched up. On the words 'Take your marks!' pull yourself up, and as the gun fires push yourself backwards and up, throwing your arms back so they enter the water first. Your body is extended with an arch in the back and your head tilted back. As your face goes under breathe out through your nose and tilt your arms up to finish the glide. Do your first stroke when you break the surface.

The longest distance you are allowed to stay underwater is 15m (50ft); only swimmers at the top level are likely to have such a long glide, but even so, it is worth learning to judge how long you stay underwater.

The backstroke start. Do not move from the coiled position (frame 2) until you hear the starter's gun. Breathe in as you push off and start to exhale as your head goes under water

TURNS

Turns are something you should practise until you can do them without thinking. For those involving underwater somersaults and rotations it is a good idea to get used to these actions by practising them in the middle of the pool. Wear goggles or a mask and use your arms to drive the motion. Breathe out through the nose – especially when somersaulting backwards!

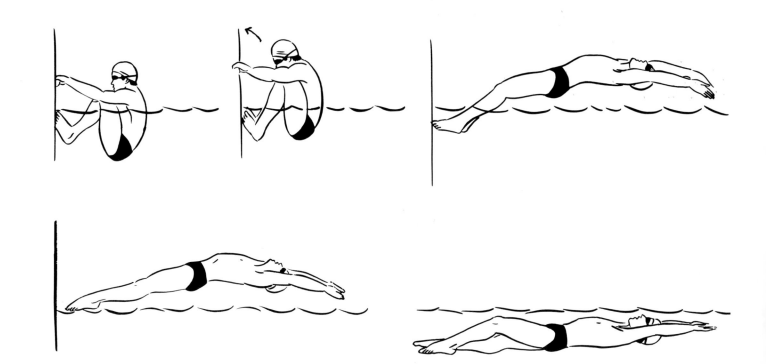

Head up turn

For the butterfly and breaststroke both hands must touch the wall at the same time and at the same level. You bring your knees up and drop one shoulder to lean away, placing both feet on the wall as you do so. As you push off your feet and turn, the leading arm goes underwater and the other arm comes over your head for the underwater glide. In breaststroke you are allowed one stroke underwater – time this to take place as the glide loses its power. Angle your arms upwards to surface.

A variation on the above turn can be used for the front crawl: you touch the wall with your leading hand and bend the elbow as you tuck your body up to bring you close to the wall for the feet placement. Take a breath as your head comes up to turn. Your other arm leads the movement through the water as you push off and sweep the leading hand over.

Tumble turn

You should learn the tumble turn for crawl since it is much quicker. As you approach the wall, complete your last stroke so that both arms are by your side and drop your head, turning your hands palm down so you can push against the water. You execute a dolphin kick to help tip your body forward and, keeping your knees bent, swing your legs up out of the water. As you come through the roll bring one arm across your body to help the quarter turn so that, as your feet touch the wall, you are sideways. Push off with your hands together, tilted upwards.

Backstroke turns

Three turns are possible for backstroke: here they are in order of speed. The simple turn is like the breaststroke turn, except that you push with your trailing arm to swing your body round, so that you are facing backwards for the push off. Your leading arm comes over your head to

This is the turn used for breaststroke and butterfly. If used for front crawl, only the leading hand would touch the wall. Remember that you cannot glide into turns or finishes, you must perform a stroke to reach the wall

The tumble turn is the most efficient turn for front crawl. The twisting motion starts once your body is tucked underwater

And they're off! The arched body position on entry can be seen clearly

Below: the jubilation of victory. Giorgio Lamberti and his Italian teammates celebrate their relay win

join the other arm which now leads the underwater glide.

In the back flip your head goes under, your back arches and your leading hand touches the wall about 30cms (1ft) below the surface. Bend your knees to bring your legs out of the water. Scull towards your head with your trailing arm to swing your body round so your feet plant on the wall on the spot which your leading hand is now leaving. Both arms go behind your head as you push off for the glide; tilt your fingers upwards and resume your stroke on surfacing. Breathe in on the last stroke before the turn and exhale through the nose as your head goes back.

The somersault turn, made legal only quite recently, is certainly the fastest. On your last stroke your recovery arm comes across your body so that your hand goes over the opposite shoulder. Your other arm completes its pull and stays in the water as you roll onto your front. Your legs come up and your arms drive the forward somersault. Bend your knees and bring them up to your chest.

As your feet touch the wall extend your arms behind you and push off into the glide. You are not allowed to kick during the turn, but may during the glide. Do not forget to breathe in before going under and breathe out through the nose during the somersault. You may not stay under water for more than 15m (50ft).

Medley turns

You need to modify some of these turns if you are competing in a medley. When changing from butterfly to backstroke it is very simple: both hands touch the wall, your legs tuck up and feet plant on the wall and you push off backwards, throwing your arms behind you. To change from breaststroke to crawl, you perform the standard breaststroke turn but must remember not to perform a stroke underwater before starting the crawl.

When switching from backstroke to breaststroke you can do the simple turn and perform a stroke underwater at the end of your glide. Or you can learn the much faster backward somersault turn: stay on your back, breathe in and, as your leading hand touches, bend the wrist so your palm is flat against the wall (the surface should be a bit rougher here to give you a grip); then bring the other hand over to a similar position on the other side of your head.

Both arms will be bent and you push off with your hands and tip back your head to start the tumble. Breathe out through your nose and tuck your legs up, planting your feet on the wall. Push off with your arms extended and fingers turned up — you will be on your front in the glide position. You are allowed one underwater stroke before surfacing. This takes a fair bit of practice but is worth learning because of its speed.

The backstroke turn. In the first three frames we see the swimmer from above; his right arm is completing the pull as his left arm comes across his body to start the roll on to his front. Frames 4 to 7 show a sideview of the forward somersault which bring his feet into contact with the wall for the push off

And remember . . .

For all turns it is important to know where to start the move, so practise during your warm-up time before the race – this is particularly important for backstroke. Use the flags which are strung above the pool at 2m (6½ft) from each end as markers and count how many strokes in from there the turn begins.

MEDLEYS AND RELAYS

Medley events are for the all-rounder. You dive in to swim butterfly, then switch to the other strokes in this order: backstroke, breaststroke and freestyle (crawl). Make sure you can perform all the turns well.

Relays are exciting to watch and compete in. It is usual to have your strongest and most determined swimmer in the final leg. You are part of a team so should feel motivated to perform well. Make sure you only dive in when your teammate has touched and that you finish your stint with a proper, legal touch.

There is no backstroke relay – just imagine the confusion at changeovers! – but there is a medley relay which starts with the backstroke and then each new swimmer performs a different stroke. In order they are: breaststroke, butterfly, freestyle.

FOLLOWING THE RULES

It is important to know all the rules governing your event before competing. In the Starts and Turns sections (pages 54–61) we have indicated what the swimmer must do to stay within the rules. It is also worth mentioning that turns and finishes must be performed at the end of a stroke; that is to say, if you are short of the wall you cannot glide and then stretch forward to touch. You must perform another complete pull, even if the recovery is short

and high to bring your head to the wall.

There are certain requirements for each stroke; here they are in short (some of these do not apply during starts and turns):

- Breaststroke – both shoulders must be level and the arms must stay underwater, both performing the same action at the same time. The arms must not pull back to waist level. The legs must also perform the same action at the same time and only the frog kick, as described in the chapter Breaststroke, may be used. Part of the head must be out of the water at all times (except when turning and starting).
- Butterfly – the arms must come out of the water during recovery. As for breaststroke, the shoulders must be level and both arm and leg actions must be identical and executed together.
- Backstroke – you must start in the water and stay on your back throughout each stroke. Easy!
- Freestyle – this means what it says so you can do what you want! Pay attention to starts, turns and finishes though.

THINKING TO WIN

If you have done all the correct preparation and training you should be in the right frame of mind as you wait for the starter's orders. Of course, you will probably be a little nervous (at least) before the start, but that is quite normal and not necessarily a bad thing – it means you will be keen to do well, and that is half of the battle.

Concentrate on your own performance, and before the start do not pay much attention to your competitors. Some of them you may already know and you may be familiar with their strengths and weaknesses; this should be information already stored in your mind which will help you plan the race – there is no need to study them now. Use the warm-up time sensibly (see page 12), getting your body ready for the activity to come. Do not forget to get familiar with the ends of the pool so you can time your turns properly.

Keep going!

There will always be the occasional gala when you do not feel at your best. It is important not to let this show — after all you do not know how your opponents are feeling or what they are thinking, and some of them might be below par as well. What is more, once the race starts you might surprise yourself; very often the excitement of the occasion will help you produce a performance you would not have expected.

Always believe you can win and be prepared to put in a final exhausting effort at the end. You should never give up, even if you are last, because this can set bad habits for the future. If halfway through a race it looks as if you cannot possibly win then concentrate on trying to set a personal best time.

If you are in second position but a long way behind, do not slacken the pace. After all, if the leader has to drop out (as sometimes happens, through injury for example) then who will be in first place? You, of course, and that position will be under threat if you have not kept up the pace.

A team sport

You should be well practised at keeping an eye on opponents during a race, so it is important to swim races in practice. It is also important, especially if you are involved in relays, to have developed a good team spirit. Try to get on with the other team members; a little healthy rivalry is no bad thing but there should not be any personal disputes between teammates. If there are problems get your coach to sort them out. So, cheer for your friends as they finish their event and urge on the clubmate swimming towards you as you crouch on the block ready to dive in and win your leg of the relay.

Don't forget

You should also think in the long term. Growth is difficult to predict — next year you might be a lot bigger and stronger and then you will be grateful for all the hard work you are doing now.

Timing judges, their thumbs on the stopwatch buttons, keep a close eye on events. Starts, turns, changeovers, strokes and finishes are all closely monitored in competitions

Acknowledgements

The Author and Publisher would like to thank the following for their very kind permission to reproduce the following illustrations:

Allsport for the photographs on pages 2–3, 27, 39, 43 (bottom).

Vandystadt/Allsport for the photographs on pages 6–7, 11, 23, 26–27, 42.

Simon Bruty/Allsport for the photographs on pages 14, 15, 30–1, 34–5, 55 (bottom), 59 (both pictures).

Bob Martin/Allsport for the photographs on page 31, 43 (top).

Tony Duffy/Allsport for the photographs on pages 46, 50–1, 55 (top), 62.

Chris Cole/Allsport for the photograph on page 47.

John Walmsley for the photograph on page 10.

Nicholas Day for all the line illustrations.

Useful addresses

Amateur Swimming Association (ASA)
Harold Fern House
Derby Square
Loughborough
Leics LE11 0AL

English Schools Swimming Association
Mr D Redman, MBE
3 Maybank Grove
Liverpool L17 6DW

Welsh Schools Swimming Association
Mrs A. E. Smith
19 Underhill Crescent
Knighton
Powys LD7 1DG

Irish Schools Swimming Association*
Mr F. Parkes
14 Finchley Park
Belfast BT4 2HZ

*includes the Republic

Scottish Schools Swimming Association
Mrs A. Dickson
10 Millburn Close
Selkirk
Border Region
Scotland

National Association of Disabled Swimmers
Solecast House
13–27 Brunswick Place
London

Index